USING THE CASE STUDY
IN TEACHING AND TRAINING

LEROY FORD

Illustrated by Joe McCormick
Based on author's original sketches

BROADMAN PRESS * *Nashville, Tennessee*

This book of pictures and words about the case study is dedicated to Judy, Daniel, and Cindy who each day present new cases requiring analysis and prescription.

© Copyright 1969. BROADMAN PRESS
All rights reserved
4234-13
ISBN: 0-8054-3413-5

Dewey Decimal Classification Number: 268.6
Library of Congress catalog card number 71-105324
Printed in the United States of America

Contents

The search for a way to express learning theory and techniques in an interesting, readable style led to the development of the cartooned-writing approach used in this and other books by the author. Most readers agree that they grasp and retain ideas better when the ideas receive exaggerated or absurd treatment through cartooning.

Most of the cartoons in this book found expression first as stick figures. Sometimes the stimulation of a class or conference session gave rise to an idea which the author later translated into stick-figure cartoons on the chalkboard. Sometimes ideas came from personal and family experiences. Significant statements in books sometimes suggested humorous nonverbal ways to express ideas.

"Cartooned writing" seeks to carry through pictures the weight of a message. Verbal symbols (words) added to the cartoons help clarify meanings and provide continuity of thought.

I wish to express appreciation to artist Joe McCormick for his assistance in sharpening the original cartoons. Phyllis Gregory kept the project moving and made helpful suggestions for improving the manuscript.

Other Books by LeRoy Ford

Primer for Teachers and Leaders
Using the Lecture in Teaching and Training
Tools for Teaching and Training
Developing Skills for Church Leaders

* * * * * * * * *

The following cartooned publications by the author are available in multi-media format (book, filmstrip, and poster series):
Primer for Teachers and Leaders
Using the Lecture in Teaching and Training
Using the Case Study in Teaching and Training

THE CASE OF METHUSELAH

Methuselah lived a l-o-o-o-o-o-o-o-ong time . . .
. . . over nine hundred years,
to be approximate!

But even so . . . he missed out on a lot of things!
He missed . . .

...THE FIRST TRIP TO
THE MOON, FOR EXAMPLE.

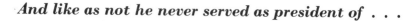

And like as not he never served as president of . . .

Even the longest-lived among us need a wider range of experiences. But time waits for no one!

We need some way to crowd more experience into our short lives.

"REMEMBER HOW SHORT MY TIME IS" (PSALM 89:47, KJV)

"REMEMBER, O LORD, WHAT THE MEASURE OF LIFE IS" (PSALM 89:47, RSV)

LET'S DEFINE "CASE STUDY"

A case study consists of an account of a problem situation, including enough detail . . . .

THE PROBLEM:

LITTLE BO PEEP
    HAS LOST HER SHEEP
AND CAN'T TELL WHERE
    TO FIND HIM!

IT'S BEEN THREE DAYS
SINCE HE WENT OUT TO GRAZE
AND NONE OF
        THE NEIGHBORS
HAVE SPIED HIM!

. . . for learners to suggest possible solutions.

POSSIBLE SOLUTIONS:

YES   NO

① SEE IF HOMEOWNER'S INSURANCE COVERS THE LOSS!

② CONTACT THE "MISSING SHEEP BUREAU!"

③ LEAVE HIM ALONE AND HE'LL COME HOME WAGGING HIS TAIL BEHIND HIM!

④ BUY ANOTHER LAMB.

⑤ REPAIR THE FENCE.

⑥ COMB THE COUNTRYSIDE WITH A HUMAN CHAIN.

Persons who prefer B I G words define the case study as . . .

SYNTHETIC ACTUALISM

(THAT MEANS A SECOND-HAND ACCOUNT OF SOMETHING THAT <u>DID</u> HAPPEN, OR ...
A FIRST-HAND ACCOUNT OF SOMETHING THAT <u>COULD</u> HAPPEN!)

Those who prefer a simpler definition call the case study a "slice of life."

In this book we will
s-t-r-e-t-c-h the definition . . .

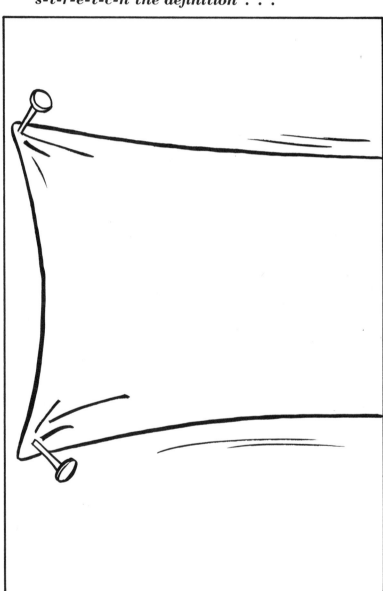

. . . to include the . . .

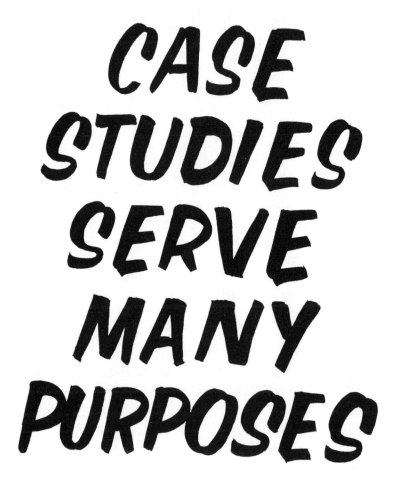

CASE STUDIES SERVE MANY PURPOSES

Teachers and leaders use the case study to . .

1. Develop skill in decision making
2. Lend reality to indirect experience
3. Pool the insights of group members
4. Focus on concrete problems
5. Help learners see many points of view
6. Show that few problems have easy answers
7. Bridge the gap between theory and practice
8. Broaden experience
9. Analyze motives
10. Present problems in proper perspective
11. Discourage "causal oversimplification"
12. Increase involvement in learning
13. Train learners to think independently as well as cooperatively
14. Give synthesis and meaning to parts of a whole

***1. Teachers and leaders use the case study to de-
velop skill in decision making.***

Some people make small decisions this way . . .

SOME PEOPLE ADD A LITTLE SUSPENSE TO DECISION MAKING BY DECIDING THIS WAY...

... AND WHEN THEY HAVE A REALLY IMPORTANT DECISION TO MAKE THEY MAKE IT THIS WAY!

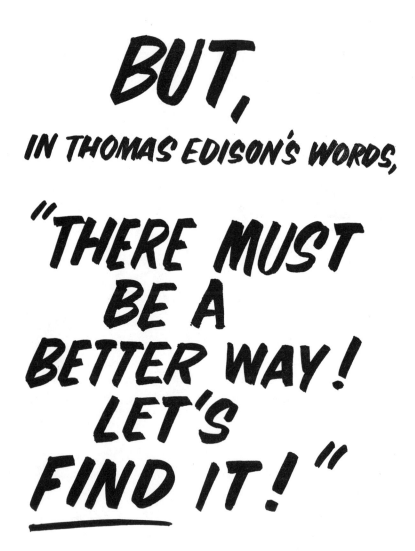

BUT,
IN THOMAS EDISON'S WORDS,

"THERE MUST
BE A
BETTER WAY!
LET'S
FIND IT!"

2. *Teachers and leaders use the case study to lend reality to experience.*
The case study doesn't put the learner in the game exactly . . .

... *BUT HE GETS ALL THE BENEFITS OF SCRIMMAGE!*

In the case study, the learner does more than read.

He does more than look at a picture. (Good as that may be!)

He sort of "climbs into the picture" himself . . .
and takes a spin!

3. *Teachers and leaders use the case study to pool the insights of group members.*

SOME PEOPLE HAVE MORE INSIGHT THAN OTHERS!

4. Teachers and leaders use the case study to focus on concrete problems . . .

For example . . .

And another example . . .

5. *We use the case study to help the learner see a problem from many points of view.*

It's like seeing the problem in a triple mirror . . .

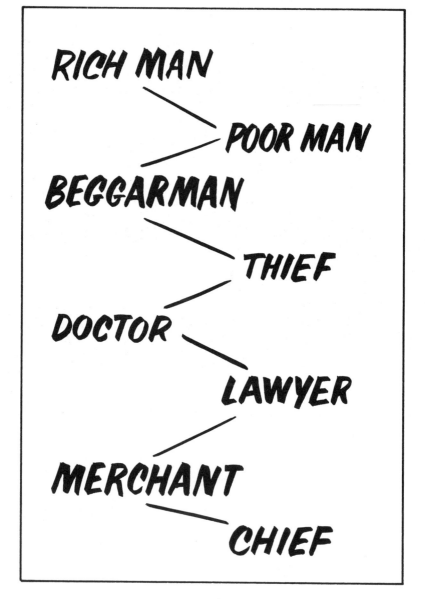

RICH MAN

POOR MAN

BEGGARMAN

THIEF

DOCTOR

LAWYER

MERCHANT

CHIEF

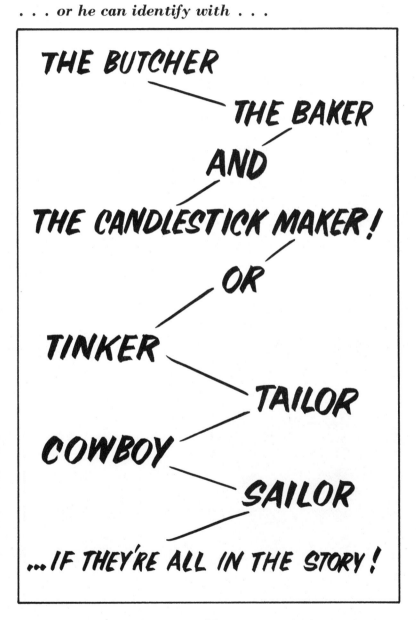

THE BUTCHER

THE BAKER

AND

THE CANDLESTICK MAKER!

OR

TINKER

TAILOR

COWBOY

SAILOR

...IF THEY'RE ALL IN THE STORY!

6. Teachers and leaders use the case study to show that few hard questions have easy answers!

Few problems have clear-cut answers—like this . . .

The answers to a great many problems look more like this . . .

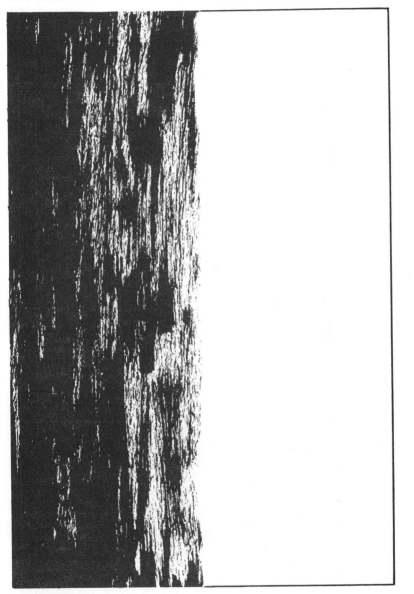

Some problems defy specific answers.

7. *Teachers and leaders use the case study to bridge the gap between theory and practice.*

A STUDENT OF BUSINESS
WITH TACT

ABSORBED MANY ANSWERS
HE LACKED,

BUT ACQUIRING A JOB,
HE SAID WITH A SOB,

HOW <u>DOES</u> ONE
FIT ANSWER TO FACT ?

From *The Case Method at the Harvard School of Business* by M. P. McNair.
New York: McGraw-Hill Book Co., Inc., 1954. Used by permission of the
publishers.

A TRAINER OF TEACHERS
NAMED HACKETT

GAVE A NEW TEACHER
A PACKET.

HE SAID,
"READ IT THROUGH!
THEY WROTE IT FOR YOU!"

BUT HE GAVE HIM
NO PRACTICE
TO BACK IT!

8. Teachers and leaders use the case study to broaden experience.

Some people crowd a little experience into a lot of time!

EXPERIENCE

. . . while others crowd a lot of experience

into a little time!

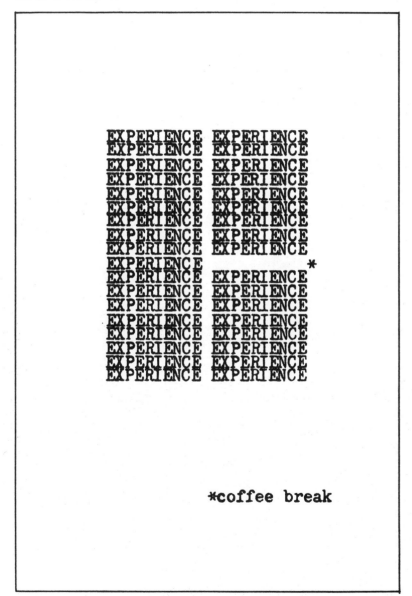

*coffee break

9. We use the case study to analyze motives.

"NO, I JUST CAN'T TEACH THAT SUNDAY SCHOOL CLASS! YOU SEE, I'VE GOT AN OLD TOM CAT IN THE ICE BOX TRYING TO MAKE A POLAR BEAR OUT OF HIM — AND I HAVE TO KEEP AN EYE ON HIM!"

Story told by Dr. J. M. Price, Sr., former dean, School of Religious Education, Southwestern Baptist Theological Seminary.

10. Some use the case study to help learners see a problem in proper perspective . . .

Some problems seem bigger than they really are!

Other problems are bigger than they seem!

11. *The case study helps learners avoid "causal oversimplification"—oversimplification of causes, if you please.*

48

12. The case study helps increase involvement—makes learning active.

13. The case study trains learners to think independently . . .

. . . as well as cooperatively.

14. *We use the case study to give synthesis and meaning to separate parts of the whole. Learners see how the parts contribute to the total effort. In BUSINESS, the learner sees how subjects like these fit into the picture:*

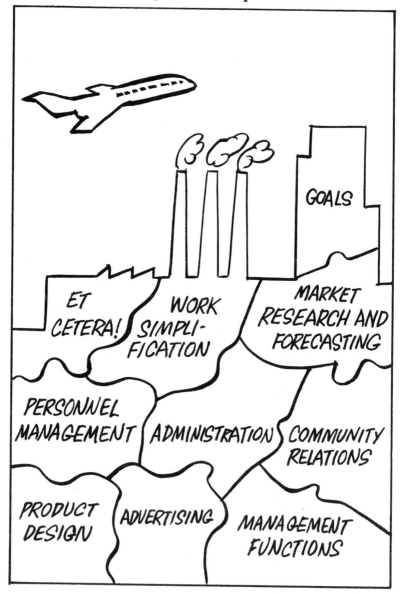

In church life, the learner sees how factors such as these, together, influence effectiveness of the church:

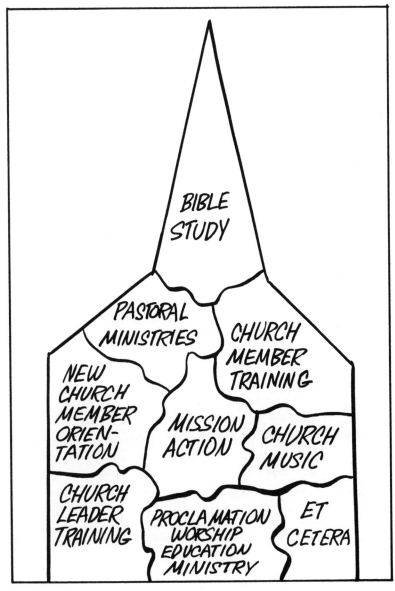

Now, just for the fun of it! Look at each key word below, and recall the purpose which it suggests.

KEY WORD   PURPOSE

1. decision _____

2. reality _____

3. insights _____

4. concrete _____

5. points of view _____

6. easy answers _____

7. gap _____

8. experience _____

9. motives _____

10. perspective _____

11. oversimplification _____

12. involvement _____

13. independent _____

14. synthesis _____

WE CAN USE CASE STUDIES IN MANY FORMS

Some Forms of the Case Study

1. Classical case

2. Unfinished story

3. "Embryo" case

4. Critical incident

5. Report analysis case

6. Cartoon teaser case

7. Informational "what-do-you-see" case

8. Psychological "what-do-you-see" case

9. "Mail basket" case

10. "Impromptu" case

11. *Ex post facto* case

12. "Baited" case

13. Educational simulation

1. The classical case study consists of a rather comprehensive record of the various kinds of evidence which influence a situation.

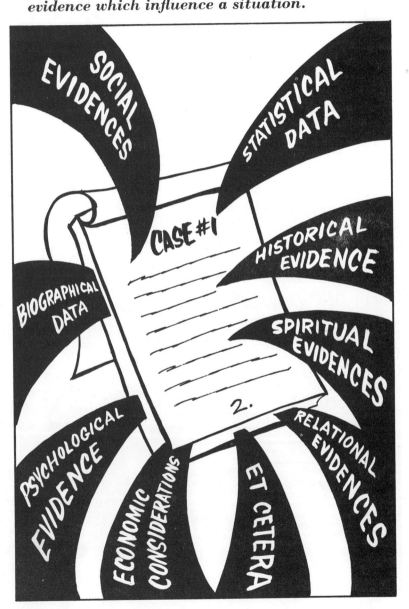

For example, the classical case would prove helpful in answering problems like these . . .

. . . and these.

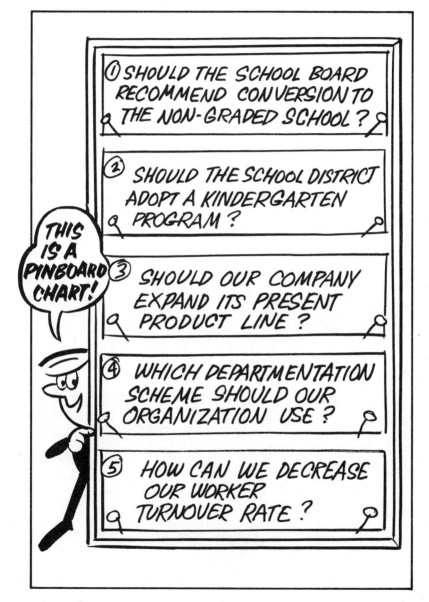

2. We can use the "unfinished stories" variation of the case study.

(the "cliff-hanger" case!)

For example . . .

What Should Donna Do?

WHEN Donna was going out the school door for recess, some of her jacks and her ball fell behind the shrubbery under the office window. While she was scrabbling around for them, she heard her teacher, Miss Redmond, talking to the principal.

"Kathy broke down and told me," Miss Redmond was saying, "that the reason she was out last week was that she and her mother went out of town to visit her father in jail."

"I really admire Kathy for telling you about it," the principal said. "What a tragic situation!"

Donna stuffed the ball and jacks into her pocket and ran over to where Janice was waiting for her. "Janice," she yelled, "I've got something to tell you!"

As Donna was telling Janice what she had overheard, some of the other third grade girls joined them and Donna let them in on what she had learned. Before long, most of the girls in the class knew why Kathy had been absent.

When the bell rang and the children lined up to go in, Kathy was right behind Janice. Janice smiled a mean smile and said:

"How's your father, Kathy? I heard you visited him last week."

One or two of the girls giggled. Kathy flushed a deep pink.

Donna sat uncomfortably through reading and science, her eyes on Kathy. Kathy hardly moved. She didn't open her workbook. She didn't write her spelling words. She just sat and stared out the window. Finally, she put her head down on her desk and simply sobbed. When Miss Redmond went to her and asked what was the trouble, Kathy choked out:

"You told. You told. All the girls know and they're all laughing."

Donna felt terrible. She had been so pleased with herself for knowing something she wasn't supposed to know that she couldn't resist the temptation to tell the other girls. The idea that Kathy might find out that everybody knew about her father had never entered Donna's head. Maybe she could do something now to make up for what she had done. But what? What should Donna do?   # #

Ask yourself:

1. Why was the girls' teasing particularly unfair to Kathy? Is teasing ever fair?

2. When a person learns a secret by accident, has he any obligation to keep it?

3. If Donna had told the secret but had made the girls promise not to let Kathy know they had heard it, would she be to blame if someone broke the promise?

From *Unfinished Stories for Use in the Classroom*, NEA Publication-Sales Section, 1201 Sixteenth Street, N.W., Washington, D.C., p. 8. Copyrighted 1966, 1968. Used with permission.

3. The "embryo" case presents just enough information to establish a problem.

GUESS WHAT! SOME OF MY GRADES AREN'T AS BAD AS SOME OTHERS!

For example . . .

---

1. Peggy watches the principal search for the keys to his car, knowing that Dick has found them. Peggy has promised not to tell.

Both case ideas adapted from *Unfinished Stories for Use in the Classroom.* See page 61.

---

2. Mary has a job of cleaning out the supply room each week. She finds herself taking home larger and larger supplies of typing paper and carbon paper.

---

4. *The "critical incident" case confronts the learner at the point of explosion in a problem. It becomes a "now-that-it-has-happened-what-do-I-do?" case.*

For example . . .

A learner finds this letter in his mailbox. What should he do?

Dear Folks,

Thank you for everything, but I am going to go to Chicago and try to start some kind of new life.

You asked me why I did those things and why I gave you two so much trouble and the answer is so easy for me to give you, but I am wondering if you will understand.

Remember when I was about six or seven and I used to want you to just listen to me? I remember all the nice things you gave me for Christmas and my birthday and I was real happy with the things for about a week at the time I got the things, but the rest of the time during the year I really didn't want presents. I just wanted, all the time, for you to listen to me like I was somebody who FELT things, too, because I remember that even when I was so young, I felt things. But you said you were busy.

Mom, you are a wonderful cook and you have everything so clean and you were so tired so much from doing all those things that made you busy, but you know something, Mom? I would have liked crackers and peanut butter just as well—if you had only sat down with me a little while during the day and said to me, "Tell me all about it so I can maybe help you understand."

And when Donna came, I couldn't understand why everybody made so much fuss because I didn't think it was my fault that her hair is curly and her teeth are so white and she doesn't have to wear glasses with such thick lenses. Her grades were better, too, weren't they?

If Donna ever has any children, I hope you tell her to just pay some attention to the one that doesn't smile very much because that one will really be crying inside. And when she's about to bake six dozen cookies, to make sure first that the kids don't want to tell her about a dream or a hope or something because thoughts are important, too, to small kids even though they don't have so many words to use when they tell about what they have inside them.

I think that all the kids who are doing so many things that grownups are tearing their hair out worrying about, are really looking for somebody that will have time to listen a few minutes and who really and truly will treat them as they would a grownup who might be useful to them. You know—polite to them. If you folks had ever said to me: "Pardon me" when you interrupted me, I would have dropped dead!

If anybody asks you where I am, tell them I have gone looking for somebody with time, because I've got a lot of things I want to talk about.

Love to all,

Jerry

From *The Kansas City Star* (Missouri), 1959. Used with permission.

*And for example . . . a person observes a superin-
tendent or a supervisor or a teacher or an officer
engaged in this bit of physical therapy!*

What should he do?

5. The report analysis case invites learners to study data in reports of various kinds.

For example, in this report, which data shows that the Sunday School teacher (1) understood boys? (2) understood his church's program? (3) knew how to visit?

Report for September 30

I called on Tom Spear whom I expect to be my leading pupil. No answer so guess he was out of town for the afternoon.

Called on Ross Jones at 1007 Castlewood Drive and waited for a while till he was done with the noon meal. Then he went with me.

First stop was at 817 Broadway where John Thomas lives. He had gone to the fair but we visited his mother and left his Sunday School book. His mother is a Baptist but her membership is elsewhere. Suggest the teacher of the thirty-year class visit her.

At 708 N. Jones, we found both parents of Grant Howard at home though the boy had gone to his grandmother's. The father is not a Christian. We left a quarterly and visited some. Suggest Mr. Johnson of the thirty-year class for men visit him.

Bill Tucker was listed as Rural Route 2. There are four routes so I had to do some inquiring. We finally located them a mile south of the city limit sign on Briggs Road. Neither parent is Christian yet. Had a good visit with them.

On the way back it came handy to stop by "The Ice-Cream Dipper." Then we went on to Burkes Drive. Harold Green did not answer but we left his book in his screen door so he could study his lesson. He lives at 314. Ronald Stroud's place proves to be farther around north of the main entrance to the subdivision but it is still called Burkes Drive. They had gone downtown. He had been in class this morning and already had his book. I only wanted to locate him so that I could find him later if necessary. Also located Spike Smith's place which locates them all.

Incidentally, we met two other boys whom we visited with but they were members of other Sunday Schools.

David V. Phillips, teacher

6. The cartoon teaser case permits learners to fill in answers to problems presented by cartoon characters.
For example . . .

7. The informational "what-do-you-see?" case serves as a stimulus to recall of information about persons, places, things, events. For example . . .

What persons and events in the history of missions do these pictures suggest?

1. _____

1. _____

8. The psychological "what-do-you-see?" case asks the learner to analyze a picture in the light of psychological factors involved. Sometimes he "reads into the picture" his own problems. For example . . .

What's the story here?

How does each person view the problem?

And another example . . .

How would each of these persons . . .

MR. HAMMOND: NEVER MARRIED; POLITICALLY LIBERAL; MEMBER TWO CIVIC SERVICE CLUBS; OWNS A CHAIN OF DRIVE-IN RESTAURANTS; GREW UP IN MIDDLE-CLASS FARM FAMILY; SIXTY YEARS OF AGE; ATTENDS CHURCH IRREGULARLY BUT HAS NEVER BEEN A MEMBER

MRS. GRANVIL: HAS NO CHILDREN; WIDOW; GREW UP IN UPPER-CLASS FAMILY; SPENDS WINTERS IN SUMMER HOME; SPONSORS AN INTERNATIONAL ART FESTIVAL; VOTES A CONSERVATIVE TICKET; FORTY-NINE YEARS OF AGE

MR. GRAYSON: GREW UP IN POVERTY; COMPLETED PH.D. IN ECONOMICS; HAS TWO TEEN-AGE SONS OF HIS OWN; SPONSORS A ROYAL AMBASSADORS' SOFTBALL TEAM; DOES VOLUNTEER SOCIAL WORK WITH A MISSION ACTION GROUP; THIRTY-FIVE YEARS OF AGE

9. *The "mail basket" case uses as case material the letters received in the daily mail. The learner makes decisions based on the nature of the correspondence.*

SOMETIMES POLICY AND PROCEDURE MAKE THE DECISION FOR HIM!

For example . . . company policy "makes the deci-
sion" in a case like this one . . .

At other times the learner must make a decision on his own—without reliance on policy or procedure. He considers the evidence and bears personal responsibility for the decision.

For example . . .

10. The impromptu case . . .
   spotlights the dynamics of the present situation

For example . . .

11. The "ex post facto" case leads toward evalu*a*-
    *tion of a decision already made. Not a "what-
    should-I-do?" case, but a "did-I-act-wisely?"
    case. The decision becomes the case!*

JUST HOW DO YOU ASSESS THE
WISDOM OF OUR DECISION? DO YOU
EVER HAVE THAT FUNNY FEELING?

12. The "baited" case deliberately withholds significant parts of the picture—or it deliberately includes insignificant parts.

13. *The educational simulation permits learners to act out their responses in direct, made-up experiences.*

IN ONE SIMULATION, LEARNERS PLAY THE ROLES OF LEGISLATORS. THEY FACE REALITY WHEN THEY TRY TO RECONCILE THEIR OWN CONSCIENCE WITH THE WISHES OF THE FOLKS AT HOME.

Some teachers and leaders use other methods and devices with the case study:

1. Brainstorming

2. Symposium

3. Small study groups

4. Listening teams

5. Debate

6. Audio and video recordings

7. Role playing

8. Films and filmstrips

9. And the most popular device of all—the written case

1. **Group members can brainstorm possible solutions to the problems the case presents.**

2. *We can ask a symposium of experts to present their analysis of the case. Then their analyses become part of the case!*

AND NOW LET'S HEAR HOW A RED CROSS WORKER WOULD SOLVE THE PROBLEM; THEN WE'LL HEAR FROM THE JAIL CHAPLAIN AND THE DIRECTOR OF THE RESCUE MISSION

3. *We can ask small study groups to analyze various aspects of a case study.*

GROUP 1: ANALYZE THE CASE FROM THE VIEWPOINT OF THE SUPERVISOR; GROUP 2: ANALYZE THE CASE FROM THE VIEWPOINT OF THE EMPLOYEE; GROUP 3: THE VIEWPOINT OF MANAGEMENT

4. We can use listening teams with the case study.

GROUP 1 WILL LISTEN FOR THE
SPIRITUAL FACTORS WHICH BEAR
UPON THE PROBLEM. GROUP 2
WILL LISTEN FOR WAYS JOHN
TRIED TO SOLVE THE PROBLEM

5. *Group members can debate any given suggested solution.*

6. *Some teachers and leaders record the case on audio or video tape for replay to a group.*

7. We can "role-play" a case study.

THAT'LL BE FORTY DOLLARS A WEEK FOR KEEPING THE HOUSE CLEAN!

8. *Some films have built-in "stops" where groups have time to discuss possible solutions. Some films have "open ends" for which learners furnish answers.*

NOW, HOW WOULD <u>YOU</u> AS A PARENT BREAK THE NEWS TO YOUR SON THAT YOU KNEW THE MODEL HE ENTERED IN THE CONTEST WAS NOT HIS?

9. *But most teachers and leaders seem to get best results when they . . .*

...DISTRIBUTE COPIES FOR STUDY IN ADVANCE

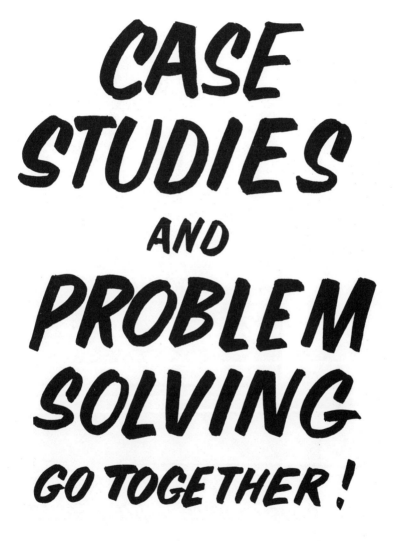

CASE STUDIES AND PROBLEM SOLVING GO TOGETHER!

Teachers and leaders need to master the steps in problem solving.

5. CHOOSE THE BETTER ONES— TAKE ACTION!

4. DETERMINE POSSIBLE SOLUTIONS.

3. FIT THE FACTS TOGETHER.

2. GET THE FACTS

1. DEFINE THE PROBLEM. (REMEMBER, A GOOD CASE LETS THE LEARNER DEFINE THE PROBLEM.)

1. *Define the problem.*

...AND POLISH IT UP LATER!

2. Get the facts!

Review the records. Remember, research serves as a tool in problem solving!

Include opinions and feelings.

AN OPINION OR A FEELING MAY NOT BE A <u>FACT</u>...BUT THE FACT THAT PERSONS HAVE OPINIONS AND FEELINGS <u>IS</u> A FACT!

3. Fit the facts together.
   Determine how one fact relates to another.

For example . . .

4. Determine possible solutions.

POSSIBLE SOLUTIONS:

YES   NO

☐   ☐   ① SEE IF SHE'S COVERED BY HOMEOWNER'S INSURANCE.

☐   ☐   ② CONTACT THE "MISSING SHEEP BUREAU."

☐   ☐   ③ LEAVE HIM ALONE AND HE'LL COME HOME WAGGING HIS TAIL BEHIND HIM.

☐   ☐   ④ BUY ANOTHER SHEEP.

☐   ☐   ⑤ REPAIR THE FENCE.

☐   ☐   ⑥ COMB THE COUNTRYSIDE.

THERE'S _THAT_ PROBLEM AGAIN!

For example . . .

5. Determine best solutions. Evaluate them one by one.

For example . . .

6. Take action! . . .

. . . case studies reduce the risk!

To secure case studies . . .

1. Look for appropriate news items in the newspaper.

2. Read the "advice" columns in the newspaper.

3. Search in professional journals and other magazines.

4. Check school textbooks—especially college textbooks.

5. Ask group members to write up some of their own experiences.

6. Write down things people say—especially things children say.

1. Read the daily papers! Watch for appropriate news items which contain case material.

2. Read the "advice" columns in the newspaper.

3. Search the professional journals . . .

For example . . .

Today's Education
National Education Association of the United States
1201 16th Street, N.W., Washington, D.C., 20036

College Management
22 West Putnam Avenue
Greenwich, Connecticut, 06830

Church Administration
127 Ninth Avenue, North
Nashville, Tennessee, 37203

. . . or the journal for your own
profession or occupation.

4. *Look in school textbooks (especially college text-books). Sometimes they contain case studies at the end of a chapter.*

5. *Ask group members to write up some of their own experiences.*

YOU MEAN THINGS THAT HAPPENED TO ME!?

6. *Write down unusual comments people make—especially those children make!*

For example . . .

DADDY, WHICH DO YOU LIKE BEST... GARDENS OR PEOPLE?

ONE
ESSENTIAL
TOOL
FOR THE
LEADER

Of all the tools of the trade, the case study leader needs the ability to probe, the ability to ask . . .

He needs the ability to ask, "Why?" . . .
. . . in a multitude of ways.

1. What seems to be the "trunk of the tree"—the real problem?

2. Which alternatives seem best?

3. What unusual or interesting thing do you see in the case?

4. Upon what data do you base your conclusion?

5. What do you think the sales manager wants to accomplish?

6. How would this action affect the department? the worker? the church? the community?

7. You ask one!

Book Summary

Methusaleh lived a l-o-o-o-o-o-o-ong time—over nine hundred years to be approximate! Just blowing out the candles on his birthday cake would take some doing! But even so, he missed out on a lot of things. He missed the first trip to the moon, for example. And like as not he never served as president of the Euphrates Valley Parent-Teachers' Association! Even the longest-lived among us need a wider range of experience. But time waits for no one. The psalmist said, "Remember how short my time is" (89:47). The Revised Standard Version says, "Remember, O Lord, what the measure of life is."

"There must be a better way. Let's find it," Thomas Edison said. We can say, "Let's find a better way to broaden experience than through use of traditional approaches." We have found a partial answer in the case study.

And that's the case for the case study.

Let's Define the Case Study

A case study is an account of a problem situation including enough detail for learners to suggest possible solutions. Doctors, lawyers, and philosophers have used case studies for years. Even nursery rhymes suggest problem situations. For example, one of them goes like this (with certain adaptations):

> Little Bo Peep
> Has lost her sheep
> And can't tell where
> To find him!
> It's been three days
> Since he went out to graze
> And none of the neighbors
> Have spied him!

Bo Peep could consider solutions such as these: (1) See if homeowner's insurance covers the loss. (2) Contact the "Missing Sheep Bureau." (3) Leave him alone and he'll come home wagging his tail behind him. (4) Buy another lamb. (5) Repair the fence. (6) Comb the countryside with a human chain.

Persons who prefer BIG words define the case study as SYN-

THETIC ACTUALISM. That means a secondhand account of something that *did* happen, or a firsthand account of something that *could* happen!

Those who prefer a simpler definition call the case study a "slice of life" that calls for diagnosis and possible treatment. In this book we stretch the definition to include the

1. Classical case
2. Unfinished story
3. "Embryo" case
4. Critical incident
5. Report analysis case
6. Cartoon teaser case
7. Informational "what-do-you-see" case
8. Psychological "what-do-you-see" case
9. "Mail basket" case
10. "Impromptu" case
11. *Ex post facto* case
12. "Baited" case
13. Educational simulation

Case Studies Serve Many Purposes

1. Teachers and leaders use the case study *to develop skill in decision making.* Some people make decisions by plucking petals from a daisy. Some people add a little suspense to decision making by drawing straws! And when they have a really important decision to make, they stack fists on a baseball bat! But "there must be a better way"!

2. Teachers and leaders use the case study *to lend reality to indirect experience.* It doesn't put the learner in the game exactly, but he gets all the benefits of scrimmage! In the case study, the learner does more than read about a problem. He does more than see a picture of it, good as that may be! In the case study, he sort of "climbs into the picture" himself.

3. Teachers and leaders use the case study *to pool the insights of group members.* Some people have more insight than others.

4. Teachers and leaders use the case study *to focus on concrete situations.* For example, the question, "What should we do about juvenile delinquency in the United States of America?" becomes "What should Joe do about his son who is on drugs?" And the

question, "How can we deal with poverty in Utopia?" becomes "How, when, and where can we conduct a literacy class for the people on Madison Street?"

5. We use the case study *to help the learner see a problem from many points of view.* It's like seeing one's self in a triple mirror. The learner can wear *all* the hats in the case. He can identify with "rich man, poor man, beggarman, thief, doctor, lawyer, merchant, chief." He can assume the role of the butcher, the baker, and the candlestick maker—if they're in the story!

6. Teachers and leaders use the case study *to show that few hard questions have easy answers!* Few problems have clear-cut answers —like black on white. More often the answers appear in shades of "gray." Some problems defy specific answers—like test questions which require the student to "define the universe and give two good examples"!

7. Teachers and leaders use the case study *to bridge the gap between theory and practice.*

8. Teachers and leaders use the case study *to broaden experience.* Some people crowd a little experience into a lot of time! Others crowd a lot of experience into a little time!

9. We can use the study *to analyze motives.* While trying to enlist a Sunday School teacher, a superintendent heard this excuse: "You'll just have to get someone else. You see, I've got an old tomcat in the icebox trying to make a polar bear out of him. I've got to keep an eye on him."

10. Some use the case study *to help learners see problems in proper perspective.* Some problems seem bigger than they are; others are bigger than they seem!

11. We can use the case study *to help learners avoid* "causal oversimplification"—oversimplification of causes, if you please.

12. Teachers and leaders use the case study *to increase involvement in learning.* No one person can monopolize the situation. Learning becomes an active process.

13. The case study trains learners *to think independently as well as cooperatively.*

14. We use the case study *to give synthesis and meaning to separate parts of the whole.* Learners experience an "ah-ha" moment when they see how related parts fit together to make a total impact. It mobilizes diverse energies in a correlated way to move

121

toward achievement of goals. The church leader sees Bible study, church member training, mission action, pastoral ministries, leader training, and church music in the light of their role in helping a church do its work in the world.

The business student sees how marketing, administration, management, and other aspects of business life contribute to achievement of goals.

Case Studies Come in Many Forms

1. *The classical case* consists of a rather comprehensive record of the various kinds of evidence which bear upon a problem. It includes such information as: social evidences, biographical data, psychological evidence, economic considerations, relational evidences, spiritual evidences, historical data, statistical information, and so on.

For example, the classical case would prove helpful in answering problems like these: Should the Missions Committee recommend a new mission project? Which curriculum should our church adopt? Should we move from our downtown location? What mission action plans does our church need? Should the school board recommend conversion to the nongraded school? Should the school district adopt a kindergarten program? Should our company expand its present product line? Which departmentation scheme should our organization use? How can we decrease our worker turnover ratio?

2. *The unfinished story* presents "cliff-hanger" cases. They usually end with "What should Joe Doe (or Jane Jones) do in this case?"

3. *The "embryo" case* presents just enough information to establish a problem. Some teachers and leaders use cases like these:

> (1) Peggy watches the principal search for the keys to his car, knowing that Dick has found them. Peggy has promised not to tell.
> (2) Mary has a job cleaning out the supply room each week. She finds herself taking home larger and larger supplies of typing paper and carbon paper.

4. *The critical incident case* confronts the learner at the explosion point in a problem. It becomes a "now-that-it-has-happened-what-do-I-do?" case.

5. *The report analysis case* invites learners to study data in reports of various kinds.

6. *The cartoon teaser case* permits learners to fill in answers to problems presented by cartoon characters. For example, two pupils tell a third pupil, "Joe, you're a tattletale if you tell Mr. Graham where we got the money!"

7. *The informational "what-do-you-see?"* case serves as a stimulus to recall of information about persons, places, things, events. For example, a picture of a cobbler viewing a map of the world could serve as a reminder of persons and events in the history of missions.

8. *The psychological "what-do-you-see?"* case asks the learner to analyze a picture in the light of psychological factors involved. Sometimes he "reads into the picture" his *own* problems. Sometimes learners interpret a picture from the viewpoint of persons with vastly different backgrounds.

9. *The "in-basket" case* is "mail in the in-basket." The learner makes decisions based on the nature of the correspondence. Sometimes policy and procedure make the decision for him! For example, if an employee wants extra vacation because of overtime work, a supervisor decides on the basis of company policy. At other times, one must base decisions on circumstantial evidence. There's no "law against it" but he must consider the circumstances. He cannot fall back on policy. He must work out a solution.

10. *The "impromptu" case* spotlights the dynamics of the present situation. The leader calls attention to problems and incidents which develop *in the group* and uses them as cases.

11. *The "ex post facto" case* leads toward evaluation of a decision already made. It becomes not a "what-should-I-do?" case, but a "did-I-act-wisely?"

12. *The "baited" case* deliberately withholds significant parts of the picture. Learners learn to search further. Sometimes a case deliberately includes insignificant material. Learners learn to "weed out" the unimportant.

13. *The educational simulation* permits learners to act out their responses to direct, made-up experiences. In one simulation, learners play the roles of legislators. They face reality when they try to reconcile their own conscience with the wishes of the folks at home!

We Can Use Various Methods and Devices with the Case Study

Many teachers and leaders use other methods and devices with the case study:

1. Brainstorming.—Group members brainstorm possible solutions to problems.
2. Symposium.—A symposium of experts present *their* analyses of the case. Then their analyses become part of the case.
3. Small study groups.—Small groups analyze various aspects of a case.
4. Listening teams.—Groups listen according to predetermined assignments.
5. Debate.—Group members debate the pros and cons of a suggested solution.
6. Audio and video tape replays.—Tape replays add reality to the case.
7. Role playing.—Role playing helps member identify more readily with a problem.
8. Films.—Some films have built-in stops where groups have time to discuss possible solutions before proceeding with the film.
9. Printed materials.—This most popular form of the case makes advance study possible.

Case Studies and Problem Solving Go Together

Teachers and leaders need to master the steps in problem solving if they expect to use the case study effectively. These steps include:

1. Define the problem.—Most leaders and group members state a "trial" problem first, and polish it up later!
2. Get the facts.—The writer of Proverbs said: "He that answereth a matter before he heareth it, it is folly and shame unto him" (18:13). We should review the records. Research serves as a tool in problem solving. Research should include facts about opinions and feelings. An opinion or a feeling may not be a *fact*—but the fact that persons have opinions and feelings *is* a fact!
3. Fit the facts together.—Facts interpreted in the light of other facts tend to suggest solutions. For example, if a church organization reports 121 enrolled, 4 in attendance, and *no* visits, one could assume that poor attendance and lack of visitation (related facts) caused the problem.

4. Determine possible solutions.—For example, when a house catches fire, occupants might call a high-level conference and consider such solutions as (1) push the panic button; (2) run for the smoke masks; or (3) evacuate the building.

5. Determine best solutions.—We should ask, How will this solution affect the individual? others? the organization?

6. Take action!—Those who train through use of the case study reduce the risks in taking action.

We Find Case Studies Where We Look for Them

Teachers and leaders find case studies in such sources as these:

1. The daily papers.—Appropriate news items many times suggest cases. For example, a headline such as this invites further attention for case use: "Rival Gangs Set for Showdown, Refuse Counsel."

2. The "advice" columns in the newspaper provide a rich source of cases.—For example, consider the possibilities in a "Dear Advisey" letter which begins like this: "We have rules around our house about how late our children can stay out. Well, the other day John, our teen-ager . . ." and so on.

3. Professional journals.—Many journals include on a regular basis one or more case studies.

4. Textbooks.—School workbooks and college textbooks frequently contain case studies at the end of chapters.

5. Group members.—Sometimes group members themselves furnish cases by writing up their own experiences.

6. What people say.—Occasionally one hears a comment which serves as a basis for a case study. For example, one child asked her father, "Daddy, tell me all about when you die. And what you don't know, just don't tell me." How should the parent answer the child?

One Essential Tool for the Leader

Of all the tools of the trade, the case study leader needs *the ability to probe*, the ability to ask, "Why?" in a multitude of ways. Questions such as these have proved helpful:

1. What seems to be the "trunk of the tree"—the real problem?
2. Which alternatives seem best?
3. What unusual or interesting thing do you see in the case?
4. Upon what data do you base your conclusion?
5. What do you think the sales manager wants to accomplish?
6. How would this action affect the department? the worker? the church? the community?

Bibliography

BIBLIOGRAPHIES OF CASES:

* Intercollegiate Case Clearing House, *Selected Cases in Business Administration*, Volume I–X, Boston: Intercollegiate Case Clearing House, Harvard Business School, Soldiers Field, Boston, Massachusetts 02163, 1967.†

* ——— *Bibliography: Cases and Other Materials for the Teaching of Multinational Business*, 1964

* ——— "Cases on Contemporary Issues," 1968

* ——— "Higher Education," 1966

* ——— "Latin America: 1966"

* ——— "Planning, Programming, and Budgeting: 1967"

* ——— "South and Southeast Asia: 1968"

* ——— "Technological Change and Automation, 1965"

Garvey, Dale M., and Garvey, Sancha K., "Simulation, Role-playing and Sociodrama in the Social Studies with an Annotated Bibliography," *The Emporia State Research Studies*, Vol. XVI, No. 2, Dec. 1967, Emporia, Kansas: Graduate Division of the Kansas State Teachers College, 1200 Commercial St., Emporia, Kansas, 66801

BOOKS:

ANDREWS, KENNETH R. (ed.). *The Case Method of Teaching Human Relations and Administration*. Cambridge: Harvard University Press, 1960.

BOCK, EDWIN A. (ed.). *Case Studies in American Government*. Englewood Cliffs, N.J.: Prentice-Hall, 1962.

† Note: The Intercollegiate Case Clearing House, Harvard Business School, has available, Fall, 1969, an Intercollegiate Bibliography of cases. Case order forms are available from Intercollegiate Case Clearing House, Soldiers Field, Boston, Massachusetts 02163.

* Bowman, Norman A. (ed.). *Woe Is Me! Case Studies in Moral Dilemmas*. Nashville: Sunday School Board of Southern Baptist Convention, 1968.

British Institute of Management. *Case Study Practice*. London: British Institute of Management, 1960.

Corsini, Raymond J. and Howard, D. (eds.). *Critical Incidents in Teaching*. Englewood Cliffs, N.J.: Prentice-Hall, 1964.

* Fallaw, Wesner. *The Case Method in Pastoral and Lay Education*. Philadelphia: The Westminster Press, 1963.

Hartshorne, Hugh and Lotz, Elsa. *Case Studies of Present-Day Religious Teaching*. New Haven: Yale University Press, 1932.

Highsmith, Richard M., *et al*. *Case Studies in World Geography*. Englewood Cliffs, N.J.: Prentice-Hall, 1961.

* Ishee, John A. (ed.). *Is Christ for John Smith?* Nashville: Broadman Press, 1968.

Lowell, Mildred Hawksworth. *The Management of Library and Information Centers*. (*The Case Method in Teaching Library Management*, Vol. I.) Metuchen, N.J.: The Scarecrow Press, 1968.

———. *The Management of Libraries and Information Centers*. (*The Process of Managing Syllabus and Cases*, Vol. II.) Metuchen, N.J.: The Scarecrow Press, 1968.

* ———. *The Management of Libraries and Information Centers*. (*Personnel Management: Syllabus and Cases*, Vol. III.) Metuchen, N.J.: The Scarecrow Press, 1968.

McNair, M. P. *The Case Method at the Harvard Business School*. New York: McGraw-Hill Book Co., 1954.

National Association of Social Workers. *The Case Method in Teaching Social Work*. New York: National Association of Social Workers, 1959.

* National Education Association of the United States. *Unfinished Stories for Use in the Classroom*. (Compilation of 44 cases from *Today's Education*.) New York: National Education Association.

Parkhurst, Charles C. *Case Studies and Problems in Business Communication*. Englewood Cliffs, N.J.: Prentice-Hall, 1960.

Pigars, Paul John William. *Case Method in Human Relations: The Incident Process*. New York: McGraw-Hill Book Co., 1961.

Society for Personal Administration. *The Case Method, a Technique of Management Development*. Washington, D.C.: Society for Personal Administration, 1957.

Sperle, Diana Henryetta. *Case Method Technique in Professional Training*. New York: Columbia University Teachers College, 1933.

The Teaching of Human Relations by the Case Method. Boston: Beacon Press, 1959.

Watson, Goodwil and Gladys. *Case Studies for Teachers of Religion*. New York: Association Press, 1926.

WILLINGS, DAVID RICHARD. *How to Use the Case Study in Training for Decision Making*. London: Business Publications, 1968.

FILMS:

Unfinished Stories (Available in 16mm and Super 8mm reel-to-reel versions and in Super 8 cartridges.). Educational Systems Division, Doubleday & Co., Dept. #8-NJ-9, Garden City, N.Y., 11530.

* Sourcebooks of case studies.